Rivers and Lakes
INSIDE OUT

Megan Kopp

🌱 CRABTREE
Publishing Company
www.crabtreebooks.com

Author: Megan Kopp
**Publishing plan research
    and series development:** Reagan Miller
Editors: Sarah Eason, Jennifer Sanderson
    and Shirley Duke
Proofreaders: Katie Dicker, Wendy Scavuzzo
Editorial director: Kathy Middleton
Design: Paul Myerscough
Cover design: Paul Myerscough
Photo research: Jennifer Sanderson
**Production coordinator and
    Prepress technician:** Tammy McGarr
Print coordinator: Katherine Berti

Written and designed for Crabtree Publishing
    by Calcium Creative

Photo Credits:

t=Top, bl=Bottom Left, br=Bottom Right

Dreamstime: Nickolayv: p. 27b; Getty Images: Hiroya Minakuchi: p. 13b;
Joel Satore: p. 23t; Shutterstock: Anatoly Tiplyashin: p. 26–27; Andrew
Zarivny: p. 24–25; BGSmith: p. 1b, p. 21b; Dean Pennala: 18–19; Ekina:
p. 15t; Filipe Frazao: p. 28b; Gleb Tarro: p: 3; Jakrit Jiraratwaro: p. 12–13;
Johnny Adolphson: p. 1, 20–21; Julian W: p, 11b; LorraineHudgins: p. 6–7;
Luna Vandoorne: p. 17b; Nemar74: 10–11; Nfoto: p.14–15; Ostill: p. 9b;
Randimal: p. 25t; SF photo: p. 16–17; Sirilipix: p. 8–9; Sky Light Pictures:
p. 4–5; Vitalii Hulai: p. 19t; Weltreisender.tj: p. 22–23, p. 28–29.

Cover: Shutterstock: Pablo Hidalgo/Fotos593; Apple2499 (br).

Library and Archives Canada Cataloguing in Publication

Library and Archives Canada Cataloguing in Publication

Kopp, Megan, author
    Rivers and lakes inside out / Megan Kopp.

(Ecosystems inside out)
Includes index.
Issued in print and electronic formats.
ISBN 978-0-7787-1499-6 (bound).--
ISBN 978-0-7787-1503-0 (pbk.).--
ISBN 978-1-4271-7659-2 (pdf).--ISBN 978-1-4271-7655-4 (html)

    1. Stream ecology--Juvenile literature. 2. Lake ecology-
-Juvenile literature. 3. Freshwater organisms--Juvenile
literature. I. Title.

QH541.5.F7K67 2015   j577.6   C2014-907855-2
                                            C2014-907856-0

Library of Congress Cataloging-in-Publication Data

CIP available at the Library of Congress

Crabtree Publishing Company
www.crabtreebooks.com   1-800-387-7650

Printed in Canada/022015/IH20141209

**Published in Canada
Crabtree Publishing**
616 Welland Ave.
St. Catharines, Ontario
L2M 5V6

**Published in the United States
Crabtree Publishing**
PMB 59051
350 Fifth Avenue, 59th Floor
New York, New York 10118

**Published in the United Kingdom
Crabtree Publishing**
Maritime House
Basin Road North, Hove
BN41 1WR

**Published in Australia
Crabtree Publishing**
3 Charles Street
Coburg North
VIC, 3058

Contents

What Is an Ecosystem?

Everything in the natural world is connected to everything else. An **ecosystem** is made up of **organisms**, the environment in which they live, and their **interrelationships**. The living things, such as plants and animals, are the **biotic factors** of the ecosystem. The **abiotic factors** include things such as soil, air, and sunlight. The biotic factors and abiotic factors rely on each other for survival.

Ecosystems Come in All Sizes

Ecosystems can be as small as a puddle in your backyard or as large as the Great Lakes. **Biomes** are large geographical areas with similar plants, animals, climates, and environments. Some of Earth's biomes include deserts, rain forests, grasslands, and tundra.

Rivers and Lakes

Water is an abiotic factor in every ecosystem on Earth. Rivers, lakes, and **wetlands** are bodies of water that have great **biodiversity**. Their waters sustain both plant and animal life, from the edges of their shores to their dark depths. A variety of **habitats** can exist alongside, and within, rivers and lakes.

Let's grab some flippers and explore the ecosystems found in the rivers and lakes of the world. As we go through this book, we will look at each ecosystem as a whole, then zoom in on one part of it.

What Is a System?

A system is a set of separate parts that work together for a purpose. Each part of an ecosystem has an important role to play. A healthy ecosystem has many different plants and animals living together. The interrelationships and connections of living and nonliving things make ecosystems strong and healthy. If any part of the ecosystem changes or fails, the other parts can be badly affected.

Mountain lakes are often the headwaters, or starting points, of rivers.

This map shows where rivers, lakes, and other biomes are found around the world.

Key

- ▪ Mountains—ranges
- ▲ Mountains—land peaks
- ▲ Mountains—sea peaks
- Forests—temperate
- Forests—taiga
- Forests—tropical
- ∿ Rivers and Lakes
- Islands

Energy in Ecosystems

All organisms need energy to survive. Energy in ecosystems comes from the sun. Organisms spread this energy in food. This is known as a **food chain**. In the food chain, there are producers, consumers, and decomposers.

Producers, Consumers, and Decomposers

Producers, such as **phytoplankton** and plants, use the sun's energy to make their own food. This process is called **photosynthesis**. Consumers cannot make their own food, so they eat the plants for energy. Animals that eat only plants and phytoplankton are herbivores. In a lake or river, herbivores include **microscopic zooplankton** and **crustaceans** such as shrimp or snails. Carnivores eat other animals. Omnivores eat plants and animals. Animals at the top of the food chain do not have **predators** hunting them. When these organisms die, decomposers release the **nutrients** back into the system.

Great blue herons are hunters and will eat everything from fish and **amphibians** to **mammals**, insects, and even other birds.

Food Webs

The energy from one food chain flows to living things in other, different food chains. When two or more food chains connect, they become a **food web**. Healthy food webs need plenty of sunshine, good soil, and a lot of water. A healthy food web has a large number of producers and fewer consumers.

Eco Up Close

The movement of Earth's water from land to sky and back is called the water cycle. Water **evaporates** from the oceans and is transported by clouds over the land. The water vapor **condenses** in the clouds and falls back to the land as **precipitation** such as rain or snow. If it lands on one side of a mountain ridge, it will flow in one direction. If it lands on the other side, it will go in a different direction. The areas of land that are drained by a river, lake, or stream are called its **watershed**. Once in the lake or river system, water flows back to the sea and the cycle begins again.

river plant → **grasshopper** → **frog** → **heron**

This food chain shows the flow of energy from one organism to another.

The Amazon River

The Amazon River starts in the Peruvian Andes and flows close to 4,300 miles (6,920 km) to the Atlantic Ocean along Brazil's coast. The Amazon River Basin is the area that feeds the mighty river. It includes the entire central and eastern area of South America, which is 40 percent of the land area of the South American **continent**.

River Full of Life

This huge river and the diversity of habitats along its length provide for a wealth of plant and animal life. The Amazon feeds the largest tropical rain forest in the world and up to 100 tree **species** have been found in a single acre of the rain forest. Close to 1,500 fish species are found in the Amazon River system. Unique mammals include the capybara, which is the world's largest **rodent**. It feeds on grasses and **aquatic** (water-living) plants along the river's edge. **Reptiles** of the Amazon include the anaconda. This water snake reaches up to 33 feet (10 m) in length. It feeds on turtles, caimans, deer, capybaras, and birds. More than 1,300 species of birds are found in the Amazon River Basin.

Challenges

The Amazon River ecosystem is being challenged by deforestation. Deforestation is when trees are cut down to clear land for other uses. When too much forest cover is lost, soil flows into the river as **sediments**. Sediments pollute the river and also destroy the river ecosystem through loss of habitats, biodiversity, and carbon dioxide removal.

Eco Focus

Deforestation affects biodiversity and it can destroy the natural habitat of organisms. It also affects the river as sediments settle on the river bed. What impact do you think the sediments have on the river and its ecosystem? What steps can be taken to limit the impact? Explain your thinking.

The Amazon's width ranges from 1.25 miles (2 km) to 6.2 miles (10 km). During the rainy season, the river can swell to 25 miles (40 km) wide with a depth of 148 feet (45 m).

Eco Up Close

The giant river otter is found only in South America along the Amazon River. Known as "river wolves," these large members of the weasel family are highly skilled predators. Their main **prey** is fish, although they will occasionally take small caimans, and crustaceans such as crabs, and snakes. Each otter can eat 6 to 9 pounds (3 to 4 kg) of food a day. Families often hunt together. As an **apex predator**, giant river otters have few natural predators. Even so, river otters are **endangered** and at risk of dying out. Although protected from hunters by law, the otters still struggle with changes to their natural habitat.

giant river otter

The Nile River

Running through 10 African countries, the Nile River is the longest river in the world. Its largest **source** is Lake Victoria. The river spreads out across a 149-mile (240-km) wide, 100-mile (160-km) long **delta**, or flat floodplain, before draining into the Mediterranean Sea in Northern Egypt. The Nile supports a wide range of ecosystems. **Tropical** rainforests and deserts fringed with grasses and reeds can both be found along its waterway.

Fish, Birds, and Hippopotamuses

Many species of fish live in the Nile River. One example is the Nile perch, which eats other fish. It can weigh up to 511 pounds (232 kg). Other species of fish in the Nile include the tiger fish, lungfish, catfish, mudfish, and eels. There are approximately 300 known species of birds along the Nile, including fish eagles, ibises, and the Nile Valley sunbird. Sunbirds feed on flower **nectar** and will eat insects. The hippopotamus, a mammal, lives in the Nile. These massive herbivores weigh thousands of pounds. Hippos are grazers that eat up to 88 pounds (40 kg) of short grass a day.

Holding Back the Water

Egypt's Aswan High Dam was built in 1970 to help stop flooding along the Nile. Before the **dam** was built, flood years were followed by **drought** with no water. The dam helps control water for crops and human settlements along the delta. The dam also stops **silt** (dirt, soil, and mud that flows in river water) from reaching the delta. Egypt now has to use **artificial fertilizers** to make up for the natural silt that used to coat the land each year following a flood.

In Egypt, the Nile River creates a lush green valley cutting through the dry desert.

10

Eco Up Close

The Nile crocodile can reach up to 20 feet (6 m) in length and weighs up to 1,650 pounds (748 kg). These carnivores eat mainly fish but will attack almost anything from birds to zebras. Nile crocodiles can eat up to half their body weight in one feeding. Young hatch from eggs and can live up to 45 years. **Overhunting** once threatened Nile crocodiles, but the species is not currently endangered.

Nile crocodile

The Yangtze River

China's Yangtze River is the third-longest river in the world, running 3,915 miles (6,300 km) from the Tibetan Plateau to the **estuary** of the East China Sea near Shanghai. The Yangtze River Basin covers an area more than four times the size of California. The river flows through many habitats as it travels from the mountains to the delta.

The Yangtze River Basin provides more than two thirds of China's total rice production. People began to grow rice in the middle Yangtze more than 11,500 years ago.

In the Upper Yangtze

The forests of the upper Yangtze provide the perfect habitat for giant pandas. Pandas need to eat 27 to 84 pounds (12 to 38 kg) of bamboo a day to survive. Pandas play an important role in bamboo forests by spreading the bamboo seeds all around the forest in their droppings.

The Lower Yangtze

The Yangtze finless porpoise lives only in the middle and lower reaches of the river. These porpoises were once apex predators but they are now threatened as a result of human-made changes in the ecosystem. Chinese alligators are found only in the lower reaches of the Yangtze. This small alligator is a carnivore. It eats fish, birds, small mammals, and other reptiles. There are 378 fish species, more than 280 mammal species, 145 amphibian species, and 166 reptile species found within the region. Industry, the building of towns, and habitat loss are affecting the health of many species in the ecosystem.

Eco Focus

The Baiji dolphin lived in the Yangtze River. In 2006, it was declared functionally extinct. This means there are too few remaining dolphins for the species to survive. Fishing practices killed most of these dolphins. How can knowledge gained from this experience be used to save the Yangtze finless porpoise? Explain your thinking.

Eco Up Close

The Yangtze finless porpoise is **critically endangered**. This means it faces a very high risk of extinction in the wild. The **population** currently stands at just 1,040 porpoises. The porpoises are carnivores, eating fish and shrimp found in the middle section of the river. **Overfishing** (taking too many fish for food) by humans is affecting their food source.

Yangtze finless porpoise

The Colorado River

The Colorado River system, including the Colorado River, its **tributaries**, and the lands that these waters drain, is called the Colorado River Basin or watershed. It drains a total of 246,000 square miles (637,137 sq km), an area almost the size of France. The river drops 14,000 feet (4,267 m) from the Rocky Mountains along the 1,450-mile (2,334-km) journey from the mountains in Colorado to the Gulf of California, passing through seven states before entering Mexico.

Through Many Zones

The river travels from **alpine** habitat and **coniferous** forests to **semiarid plateaus** and deep desert canyons. The river then travels on through desert to the delta, emptying into the ocean. The river passes through many different zones, so the basin has great biodiversity. The ecosystem around the river is home to 1,500 plant species and 355 different bird species.

Using the River's Water

The Colorado no longer runs free. More than 20 dams have been built on the Colorado River and its tributaries for flood control, to create **hydroelectricity** (electricity produced from water), to store water for agriculture and other human uses, and to use the river's varying flows to create a steady water supply for people and crops. Around 85 percent of the Colorado River's annual flow now comes from **snowmelt** in the Rocky Mountains. **Climate change** is also causing a hotter, drier environment.

It is estimated that water flow in the Colorado River Basin will be reduced by around 10 to 30 percent by 2050 due to human intervention. Already, the Colorado no longer regularly reaches the sea.

tamarisk

Eco Up Close

Tamarisk, or salt cedar, was first planted in the 1800s for erosion control. This **invasive species** spread rapidly along the Colorado River system. In ideal conditions, the shrub can live 75 to 100 years. It produces up to 500,000 seedlings each year. The lightweight seeds are easily **dispersed**, or scattered, by wind and water. Each plant consumes large amounts of water. Tamarisk easily **outcompetes native** plant species. Its huge root systems make riverbanks harder and less likely to erode. This causes the channel to narrow as sediment builds up. Narrow channels increase the speed and the destructive nature of the river during floods.

The St. Lawrence River

The St. Lawrence River is the only natural outlet to the Great Lakes. This huge river connects the Great Lakes to the Atlantic Ocean. The St. Lawrence has a drainage basin of more than 386,102 square miles (1,000,000 sq km).

The River Home

The St. Lawrence River is home to more than 80 different species of fish including muskellunge, northern pike, walleye, largemouth bass, smallmouth bass, yellow perch, rock bass, black crappie, and pumpkinseed and bluegill sunfish. Some of the fish feed on the microscopic zooplankton found in the waterway. Bald eagles are apex predators along the river, feeding on the many different species of fish. American eels are snake-like fish, eating everything from small fish to insects and dead animal matter. They are part of the river's cleanup crew. In the 1980s, 1 million eels **migrated**, or traveled, up the river. By 2013, there were 40,000. Habitat loss and overfishing are two of the reasons for this decline.

Rich with Plant Life

The river ecosystem contains a wide variety of plant life. It ranges from taiga in the upper sections of the river to riverbank grasses along the middle sections and **salt-tolerant** plants in the estuary. Migrating ducks and geese rely on these plants as food sources.

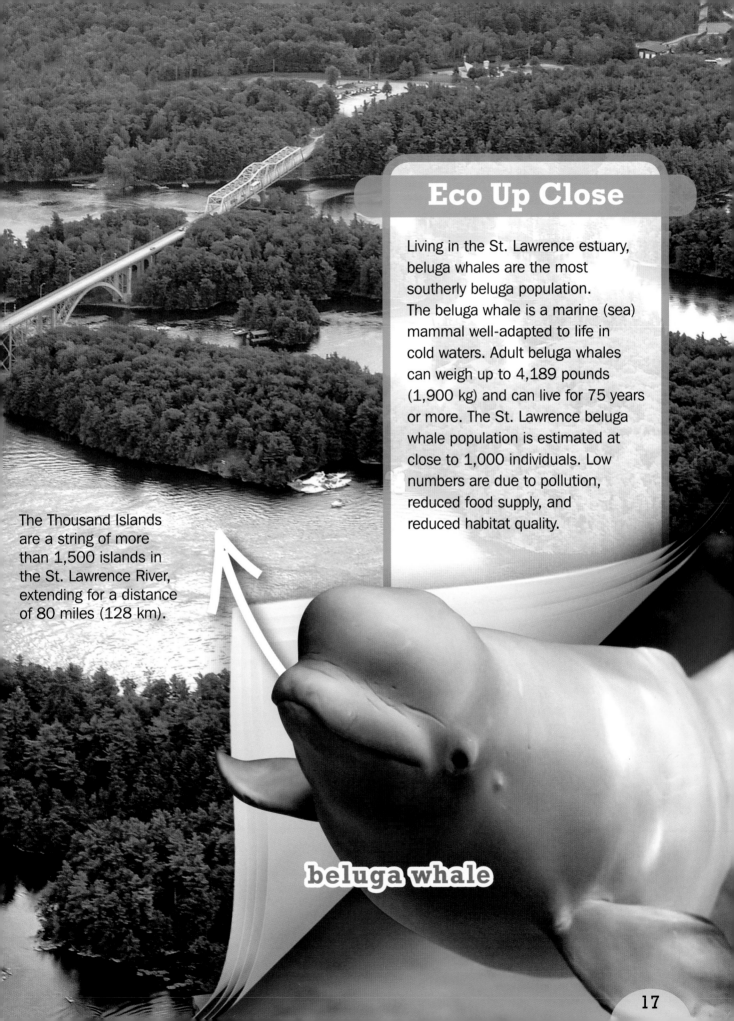

Eco Up Close

Living in the St. Lawrence estuary, beluga whales are the most southerly beluga population. The beluga whale is a marine (sea) mammal well-adapted to life in cold waters. Adult beluga whales can weigh up to 4,189 pounds (1,900 kg) and can live for 75 years or more. The St. Lawrence beluga whale population is estimated at close to 1,000 individuals. Low numbers are due to pollution, reduced food supply, and reduced habitat quality.

The Thousand Islands are a string of more than 1,500 islands in the St. Lawrence River, extending for a distance of 80 miles (128 km).

beluga whale

The Great Lakes

The Great Lakes include Lake Superior, Lake Michigan, Lake Huron, Lake Erie, and Lake Ontario. These lakes and their connecting channels form the largest freshwater system on Earth. Altogether, they contain about 5,500 cubic miles (22,925 cubic km) of water. They cover a total area of 94,250 square miles (244,106 sq km). They hold more than 84 percent of North America's freshwater supply.

Only Lake Baikal is greater by volume than the combined Great Lakes.

Great Ecosystems

Although the lakes are massive, their ecosystem functions the same as any other. Sunlight provides the abiotic factors of heat and energy. Phytoplankton use sunlight for photosynthesis. Zooplankton eat the phytoplankton. Small fish eat the zooplankton. Big fish eat smaller fish. Within the waters of the Great Lakes, there are 180 different types of native fish. The largest fish is the lake sturgeon, which can grow to more than 6.5 feet (2 m) long.

Moose, beavers, and river otters are just a few of the mammals relying on the wetlands around the Great Lakes. The lakes are also important **breeding**, feeding, and resting areas for birds such as the bald eagle, common loon, double-crested cormorant, common tern, least bittern, and common merganser.

Eco Focus

Lake Erie and Lake Ontario are believed to be the most polluted of the Great Lakes. They are small, have many people living around them, and are the last lakes in the chain. Some of the pollution from the upstream lakes ends up there. Pollution comes from many sources. Some of it has been in the system for decades. Why would it be important to clean up the lakes? Could they just be left to flush themselves out over time? Explain your thinking.

zebra mussel

Eco Up Close

Zebra mussels are native to southern Russia. They were introduced to the Great Lakes by foreign ships. They spread rapidly. Zebra mussels now exist in many aquatic systems in the eastern United States. They are expected to invade fresh waters throughout the entire East Coast of the United States. Zebra mussels outcompete other **filter feeders** for food. Filter feeders are animals that feed by straining food particles from water. Zebra mussels smother clams, native mussels, and snails. They also clog pipes for facilities such as power plants. Once zebra mussels become established in an area of water, they are impossible to remove completely.

Great Salt Lake

Great Salt Lake is the largest natural lake west of the Mississippi River. It is the remains of a great lake from the ice age that took place 30,000 years ago. As the **climate** dried after the ice age, the lake shrunk to become Great Salt Lake. The first scientific measurements of the lake's level were taken in 1849. Since then, the level has changed by 20 feet (6 m). In some places, the shoreline has moved as much as 15 miles (24 km). Today, the lake is approximately 75 miles (121 km) long and about 35 miles (56 km) wide.

Salty Lake

Great Salt Lake is salty because it does not have an outlet to the ocean. Tributaries of the lake bring in small amounts of salt dissolved in their freshwater flow. Once in the lake, most of the water evaporates leaving the salt behind. The water levels of Great Salt Lake are affected by changes in flows into the lake. The lake is located in a broad, flat basin so there is more evaporation due to a greater surface-area-to-volume ratio. Great Salt Lake is too salty to support fish and most other aquatic species, but several types of algae live in the lake. Brine shrimp and brine flies have adapted to the high salt levels and feed on the algae. Biologists have estimated the brine fly population to be more than 100 billion. Much of the lake is ringed by wetlands, making Great Salt Lake one of the most habitable places for migrating and nesting birds.

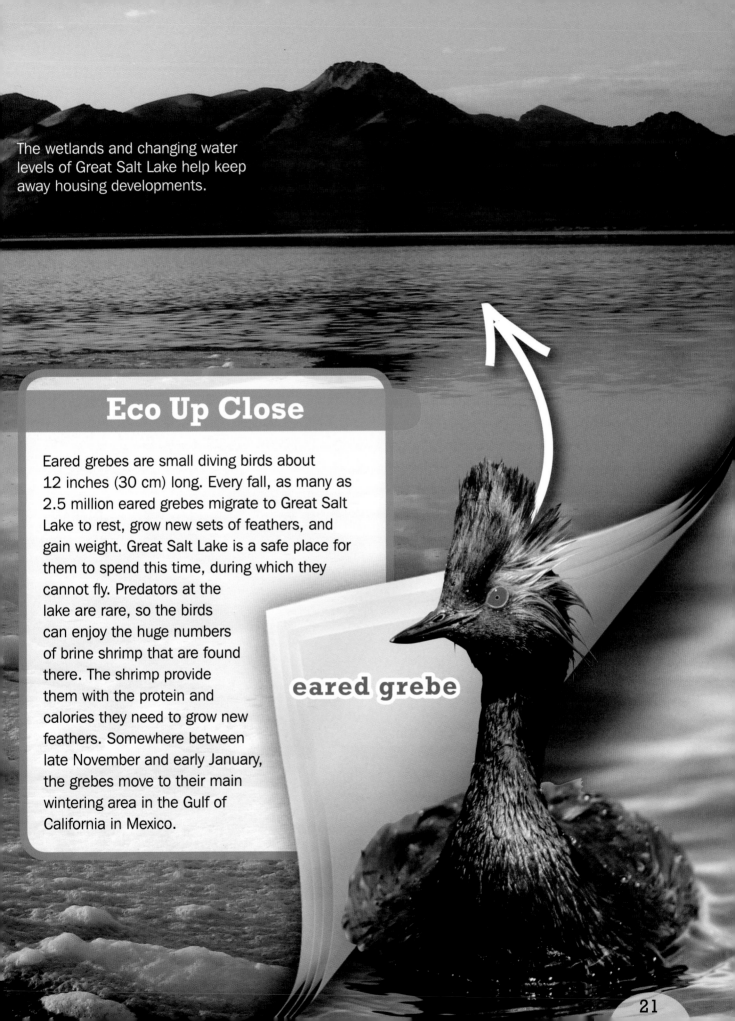

The wetlands and changing water levels of Great Salt Lake help keep away housing developments.

Eco Up Close

Eared grebes are small diving birds about 12 inches (30 cm) long. Every fall, as many as 2.5 million eared grebes migrate to Great Salt Lake to rest, grow new sets of feathers, and gain weight. Great Salt Lake is a safe place for them to spend this time, during which they cannot fly. Predators at the lake are rare, so the birds can enjoy the huge numbers of brine shrimp that are found there. The shrimp provide them with the protein and calories they need to grow new feathers. Somewhere between late November and early January, the grebes move to their main wintering area in the Gulf of California in Mexico.

eared grebe

Lake Mead

Lake Mead is a human-made **reservoir** formed when a dam blocked the Colorado River near Las Vegas, Nevada. Lake Mead's original **elevation** is 1,221 feet (372 m). At this height, the reservoir covers about 248 square miles (642 sq km). It runs about 110 miles (177 km) east toward the Grand Canyon and about 35 miles (56 km) up the Virgin River. At its widest point, Lake Mead can be 8 miles (13 km) wide.

The white cliffs along Lake Mead's shoreline show how the water level has dropped over time.

Demand and Drought

At its normal elevation, Lake Mead would contain approximately 326,000 gallons (1,234,044 l) of water. The reservoir can store enough water to cover the entire state of Pennsylvania with 1 foot (30 cm) of water. The water level of Lake Mead has dropped significantly in recent years. Increased water demand and an ongoing period of drought are the main reasons for this.

Lake for Life

The Lake is important for sustaining mammals such as plant-eating bighorn sheep and their predator, the mountain lion. Although it is still a desert environment, the creation of Lake Mead attracted many different species of water birds and shore birds. The **vegetation** (plantlife) along the shorelines has also become a breeding ground for insect-eating birds.

Eco Focus

Although dams and reservoirs provide enormous benefits for human populations, they can also threaten water supplies. More than one tenth of the flow in the Colorado River evaporates every year in reservoirs along its path. How might this affect the ecosystems that depend on the river? Explain your thinking.

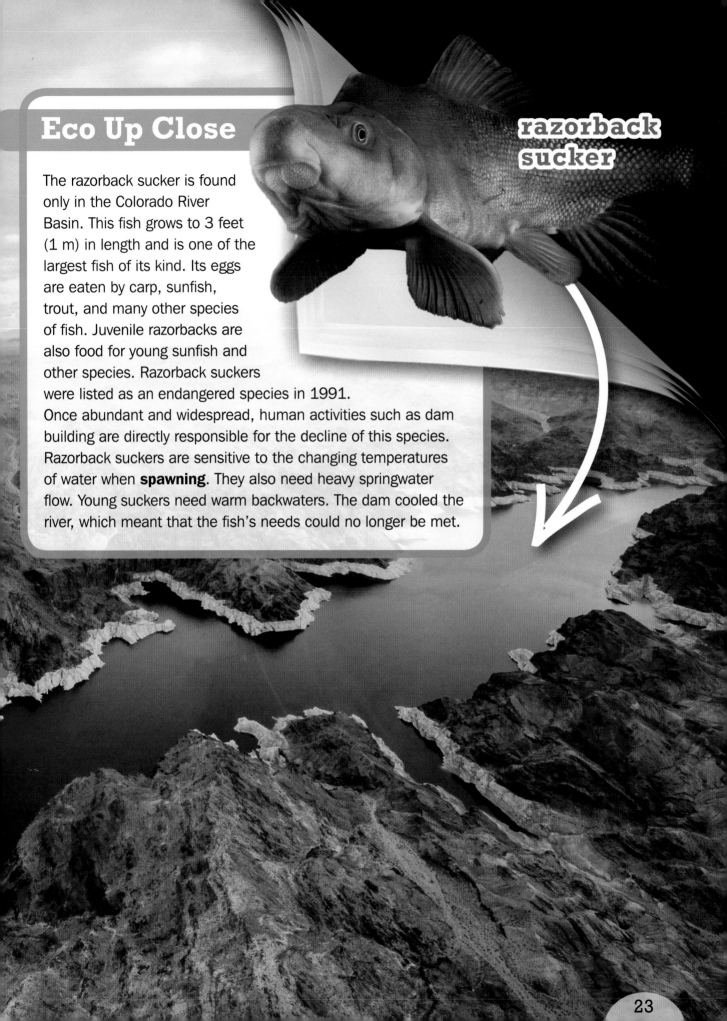

Eco Up Close

razorback sucker

The razorback sucker is found only in the Colorado River Basin. This fish grows to 3 feet (1 m) in length and is one of the largest fish of its kind. Its eggs are eaten by carp, sunfish, trout, and many other species of fish. Juvenile razorbacks are also food for young sunfish and other species. Razorback suckers were listed as an endangered species in 1991.

Once abundant and widespread, human activities such as dam building are directly responsible for the decline of this species. Razorback suckers are sensitive to the changing temperatures of water when **spawning**. They also need heavy springwater flow. Young suckers need warm backwaters. The dam cooled the river, which meant that the fish's needs could no longer be met.

Crater Lake

Crater Lake is located in the Cascade Range of southwestern Oregon. It formed during the collapse of Mount Mazama 7,700 years ago. Crater Lake is a caldera, which is a volcanic feature usually formed by the collapse of land after a volcanic eruption. Crater Lake is about 6 miles (10 km) in diameter and is close to 2,000 feet (610 m) deep. It is the deepest lake in the United States. It is fed by rain and snowfall rather than a stream or river.

Lake Living

There are no other bodies of water connected to Crater Lake. All of its water comes from precipitation. So, as a result, the lake has high levels of dissolved salts. The lack of connection to other bodies of water also means that it does not have any native species of fish. However, it does have introduced species of trout and salmon. The pine and fir forest area around the lake is home to deer, bears, eagles, hawks, owls, and grouses. Amphibian species such as the long-toed salamander breed in the lake. Eggs are laid in the water. Larvae can spend another full year in the lake before growing legs and moving onto land. The Crater Lake newt is found only in the Crater Lake caldera.

Eco Focus

Ecosystems such as Crater Lake change when non-native species are introduced. Trout and salmon species are popular for fishermen, but they are predators of native amphibians. What are the pros and cons of bringing non-native species to protected areas such as Crater Lake? Explain your thinking.

long-toed salamander

Eco Up Close

Long-toed salamanders have two different life phases. Larvae hatch and live in the lake, where they feed on tiny water crustaceans, or zooplankton. As they grow, larvae prey on **invertebrates** (animals with no backbones), tadpoles, and other smaller salamander larvae. The aquatic larvae change into four-legged adult salamanders and return to land. They live on the shores of the lake. The adults prey on small invertebrates including worms, insects, and spiders. In turn, both adults and larvae are food for insects, birds, fish, bullfrogs, and garter snakes. When threatened, adult salamanders ooze a sticky substance from their skin that tastes so awful that predators will not attack them.

The water of Crater Lake is very clear because of the absence of pollutants. It is possible to see to a depth of more than 100 feet (30 m).

Lake Baikal

Lake Baikal is the deepest lake in the world. It is also the biggest by volume. The lake is 395 miles (636 km) long and averages 30 miles (49 km) wide. Lake Baikal has 1,300 miles (2,092 km) of shoreline and it holds about one fifth of Earth's fresh water. Located in southeast Siberia in Russia, Lake Baikal is 25 million years old. The lake is so old and so isolated that it is one of the richest freshwater habitats. In fact, it is sometimes known as the "Galápagos of Russia." More than 330 rivers and streams feed the lake.

In the Depths, at the Surface

In Lake Baikal, there are between 1,500 and 1,800 animal species at different depths. There are also hundreds of plant species living on or near the lake surface. Most of these species are found only in Lake Baikal and are **endemic**. Golomyanka is an endemic species of fish found in Lake Baikal. These fish do not lay eggs. Instead, they give birth to live young. More than 320 bird species are also found in the Lake Baikal area.

The Problem of Global Warming

Global warming is affecting Lake Baikal. Currently, the lake freezes over in January and thaws in May or June. As temperatures rise, the ecosystem responds to the change. Shorter periods of ice cover slow the growth of the lake's algae.

While the ice on Lake Baikal has usually melted by June, sometimes blocks of ice can be seen drifting on its surface as late as July.

Eco Focus

Algae is the main food for the many crustaceans living in Lake Baikal. Crustaceans are food for the fish. How would global warming continue to affect a northern lake ecosystem? How would the ecosystem change? Explain your thinking.

Eco Up Close

The Baikal seal is a uniquely freshwater species found only in Lake Baikal. Locals call it the nerpa. In early spring, pregnant females move onto the ice where they build an ice den in which their pup is born. Newborns have white coats so they are camouflaged, or hidden, on the ice. They do not enter the water until they are two to three weeks old. The seals feed mostly on fish such as bullheads and golymanka. Each adult seal eats about 6.5 pounds (3 kg) of fish a day. The Baikal seal is at the top of the lake's food chain.

Baikal seal

All Part of a System

Of all the water found above, on, and below Earth's surface, 97.5 percent of it is salt water. Only 2.5 percent exists as fresh water. More than two thirds of this fresh water is in the form of ice and permanent snow. In reality, only 31 percent of the fresh water exists as fresh groundwater. Of this 31 percent, only 24 percent can be found in lakes, reservoirs, and river systems!

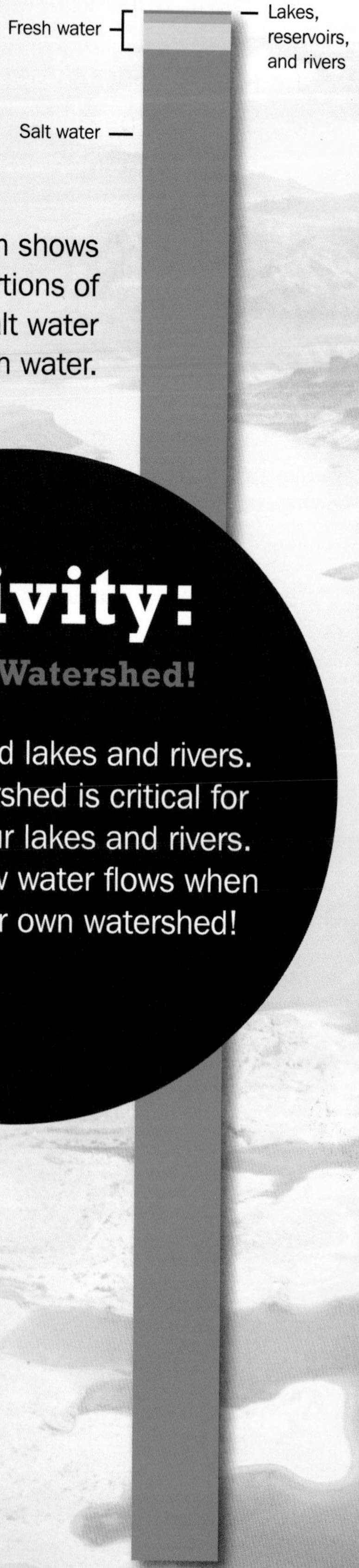

Fresh water

Salt water

Lakes, reservoirs, and rivers

This diagram shows the proportions of Earth's salt water and fresh water.

From Sky to Sea

Water is always moving, and it follows the water cycle from the sky and watersheds to the sea and back again. Watersheds can be large or small. They can be found in wild places and urban spaces. What happens in watersheds affects everything downstream. Watersheds can easily be polluted by industrial waste, runoff from farming, and sewage. Deforestation also has an impact on watersheds. We rely on watersheds for all of our water needs. We need to care for watersheds to protect our freshwater resources.

Activity:
Create a Watershed!

Watersheds feed lakes and rivers. A healthy watershed is critical for the health of our lakes and rivers. You can see how water flows when you create your own watershed!

Instructions

1. Take the sheet of graph paper and loosely crumple it.
2. Uncrumple the paper (be careful not to flatten it out too much) and set it on the cardboard.
3. Carefully tape down the edges of the paper to the cardboard, leaving at least 1 inch (2.5 cm) of the cardboard exposed around the edge.
4. Look at an example of a plastic relief map, if you have one. If you do not have one, you could ask an adult to search for an example of one on the Internet.
5. Using a dark-colored marker, carefully shade the tops of your paper "mountains" and ridges. Note that these ridges are the boundaries of watersheds.
6. Using the blue marker, carefully draw where you think the rivers and lakes would be in your "valleys."
7. Using the spray bottle, mist the paper watershed. Observe how the water seeps or flows downhill. Heavy spray will create "lakes."
8. Did you correctly predict where the lakes and rivers would be in your model?

You Will Need:

- Sheet of graph paper
- Sheet of cardboard, about the same size as the graph paper
- Several different colors of washable, dark-colored felt markers, including one blue marker
- Spray bottle filled with tap water
- Clear tape
- Example of relief map, in plastic or on an Internet site

step 1   **step 3**

step 7

The Challenge

Rivers and lakes rely on their watersheds. Once your experiment is complete, present it to others and discuss the following questions:

- How big were the watersheds for your lakes and rivers?
- Were they larger than you expected?
- What do you think would happen if that watershed was polluted?
- How would this affect the lake and river ecosystems?
- What can be done to limit this impact?

Glossary

Please note: Some bold-faced words are defined in the text

abiotic factors Nonliving parts of an ecosystem, such as water and soil

alpine The area above the treeline

amphibians Animals such as frogs and salamanders that begin life in water, then live on land as adults

apex predator An animal at the top of the food chain, which has few, if any, predators of its own

artificial fertilizers Human-made substances that are added to soil to add nutrients and help the growth of plants

biodiversity The variety of plant and animal life in an ecosystem or other area on Earth

biotic factors Living parts of an ecosystem, such as plants and animals

breeding Producing offspring

climate The normal weather in a specific area

climate change A process in which the environment changes to become warmer, colder, drier, or wetter than normal. This can occur naturally, or it can be caused by human activity

condenses When water vapor cools and changes to liquid form

coniferous Describing an evergreen tree that produces cones and has needles or scale-like leaves

continent A landmass, or large area of land, such as North America, Asia, or Australia

crustaceans Animals, such as crabs and shrimp, that live in water and have a hard shell and a segmented body

dam A structure that blocks the flow of water in a river or stream

delta A triangle-shaped piece of land that forms when a river flows into an ocean and the sediments carried by the river are dropped and build up

drought When the land becomes very dry because no rain has fallen for a long time

ecosystem A group of living and nonliving things that live and interact in an area

elevation Height of a location

endangered At risk of dying out

endemic Found only in one country or area

estuary The tidal mouth of a large river and the transition zone from fresh water to salt water

evaporates When water is heated by the sun and changed from a liquid into a gas called water vapor

food chain A chain of organisms in which each member uses the member below as food

food web The interlinked food chains in an ecosystem

habitats The natural environments of animals or plants

interdependent Relying on each other for survival

interrelationships The relationships between many different organisms and their environment

invasive species A species that is introduced into an ecosystem where it did not originally live, often causing harm

mammals Warm-blooded animals that have lungs, a backbone, and hair or fur, and drink milk from their mothers' body

microscopic So small that it can be seen only through a microscope

migrated Traveled to another area for food or to reproduce

native Originating from a specific location

nectar A sweet liquid found in some flowers

nutrients Substances that allow organisms to thrive and grow

organisms Living things

outcompetes Is more successful than another competing for the same thing

overhunting Hunting too many of one species

photosynthesis The process in which plants use sunlight to change carbon dioxide and water into food and oxygen

phytoplankton Microscopic organisms that are able to produce their own food through photosynthesis

plateaus Areas of high, level ground

population The total number of a species in an area

precipitation Water that falls from the clouds as rain, snow, sleet, or hail

predators Animals that hunt other animals for food

prey An animal that is hunted by another animal for food

reptiles Animals, such as lizards and snakes, that have scales and that rely on the surrounding temperature to warm or cool their bodies

reservoir An artificial lake that is used to store a large supply of water for use in people's homes and in businesses

rodent A small animal that has sharp front teeth

salt-tolerant Able to grow in salty water

sediments Dirt, sand, or soil that is carried away by fast-moving water, and falls to the bottom of a body of water when the flow slows down

semiarid Dry regions that are not dry enough to be considered a desert

snowmelt Water from melting snow

source The start of a river

spawning Producing or laying eggs in water

species A group of animals or plants that are similar and can produce young

tributaries River or streams that flow into a larger river or lake

tropical Describing a hot and humid climate

wetlands Shallow ponds or stretches of muddy land where water soaks the ground

zooplankton Microscopic floating or swimming animals that are part of the plankton food supply that all water organisms live on

Learning More

Find out more about Earth's precious river and lake ecosystems.

Books

Baker, Nick. *Rivers, Ponds and Lakes* (Habitat Explorer). San Francisco, CA: HarperCollins Publishers, 2006.

Callery, Sean. *Life Cycles: River*. New York, NY: Kingfisher, 2013.

Johnson, Robin. *The Mississippi: America's Mighty River* (Rivers Around the World). Ontario, Canada: Crabtree Publishing Company, 2010.

Websites

Visit the website below to learn about some of the careers you could choose in ecology:
http://kids.nceas.ucsb.edu/ecology/careers.html

Discover more about the science of freshwater biomes at:
www.ducksters.com/science/ecosystems/freshwater_biome.php

Read more freshwater facts at:
http://kids.nceas.ucsb.edu/biomes/freshwater.html

Dive into this site to learn more about lakes:
www.mbgnet.net/fresh/lakes/index.htm

Index